CRYSTAL LAKE PUBLIC LIBRARY

W9-BCP-087

W 7/16

DISCARD

JA - - '15

PROPERTY OF CLPL

Rabbits

Wil Mara

Cavendish Square
New York

Published in 2014 by Cavendish Square Publishing, LLC
303 Park Avenue South, Suite 1247, New York, NY 10010

Copyright © 2014 by Cavendish Square Publishing, LLC

First Edition

No part of this publication may be reproduced, stored in a retrieval system, or transmitted in any form or by any means—electronic, mechanical, photocopying, recording, or otherwise—without the prior permission of the copyright owner. Request for permission should be addressed to Permissions, Cavendish Square Publishing, 303 Park Avenue South, Suite 1247, New York, NY 10010. Tel (877) 980-4450; fax (877) 980-4454.

Website: cavendishsq.com

This publication represents the opinions and views of the author based on his or her personal experience, knowledge, and research. The information in this book serves as a general guide only. The author and publisher have used their best efforts in preparing this book and disclaim liability rising directly or indirectly from the use and application of this book.

CPSIA Compliance Information: Batch #WW14CSQ

All websites were available and accurate when this book was sent to press.

Library of Congress Cataloging-in-Publication Data

Mara, Wil.
Rabbits / by Wil Mara.
p. cm. — (Backyard safari)
Includes index.
ISBN 978-1-62712-310-5 (hardcover) ISBN 978-1-62712-311-2 (paperback) ISBN 978-1-62712-312-9 (ebook)
1. Rabbits — Juvenile literature. I. Mara, Wil. II. Title.
SF453.2 M28 2014
599.32 PET—dc23

Editorial Director: Dean Miller
Senior Editor: Peter Mavrikis
Copy Editor: Cynthia Roby
Art Director: Jeffrey Talbot
Designer: Joseph Macri
Photo Researcher: Alison Morretta
Production Manager: Jennifer Ryder-Talbot
Production Editor: Andrew Coddington

The photographs in this book are used by permission and through the courtesy of: Cover by Margaret S Sweeny/Flickr Open/Getty Images; Milk & Honey Creative/Brand X Pictures/Getty Images, 4; Andrew Howe/Vetta/Getty Images, 6; © iStockphoto.com/Shaiith, 7; Stuart Franklin/Staff/ Getty Images Sport/ Getty Images, 8; Leonard Lee Rue III/ Photo Researchers/Getty Images, 9; James H Robinson/Photo Researchers/Getty Images, 10; Leonard Lee Rue III/ Photo Researchers/Getty Images, 11; Nature Picture Library/Britain On View/Getty Images, 12; Cheyenne Montgomery/Flickr/Getty Images, 13; David De Lossy/Photodisc/Getty Images, 14; Cusp/SuperStock, 15; Radius Images/Radius Images/Getty Images, 16; BSIP/Contributor/Universal Images Group/Getty Images, 17; Ed Reschke/Oxford Scientific/Getty Images, 18; Margaret S Sweeny/Flickr Open/Getty Images, 19; Joel Sartore/National Geographic, Getty Images, 20; Juniors/SuperStock, 21; John Cancalosi/Peter Arnold/Getty Images, 22; NHPA/SuperStock, 22; Visuals Unlimited, Inc./Neal Mischler/Visuals Unlimited/Getty Images, 22; Stan Osolinski/Oxford Scientific/Getty Images, 22; PhotoAlto/James Hardy/PhotoAlto Agency RF Collections/Getty Images, 24; Robert Daly/Caiaimage/Getty Images, 25; Comstock/ Comstock Images/Getty Images, 26; NHPA/SuperStock, 27; Biosphoto /SuperStock, 28.

Printed in the United States of America

Contents

Introduction

Have you ever watched a squirrel chasing another squirrel around a tree? Or a group of deer leaping gracefully through a stretch of winter woods? If you have, then you know how wonderful it is to discover nature for yourself. Each book in the Backyard Safari series takes you step-by-step on an easy outdoor adventure, and then helps you identify the animals you've found. You'll also learn ways to attract, observe, and protect these valuable creatures. As you read, be on the lookout for the Safari Tips and Trek Talk facts sprinkled throughout the book. Ready? The fun starts just steps from your back door!

ONE

A Rabbit's Life

Their Bodies

Many people think of rabbits as "cute little animals"—and they are! Their bodies are oval shaped with a little tail at the back that matches the rest of their body color. However some rabbits, such as the cottontail rabbit, also have a white underside. Wild rabbits are covered in long, soft fur that can range in colors from various shades of brown or gray to a creamy off-white. Most adult rabbits grow to between 8 and 12 inches long (20 to 30 cm), although there are some species that can reach up to 20 inches (51 cm). They usually weigh

Trek Talk
Because of the way their eyes are positioned, rabbits can see what is behind them without turning their heads. However, they have a blind spot straight in front of them!

about 2 to 4 pounds (1 to 2 kg), although a few species grow heavier than that. They have large round eyes that are most commonly a rich brown color, although a few species have eyes of either blue or gray. Their tiny, v-shaped noses are framed on each side by sets of stiff whiskers. Their ears are quite long in relation to the rest of their bodies. Most will grow to a maximum of 5 or 6 inches (13 to 15 cm), although in a few cases they can be much longer. Their hind legs are longer and more powerful than their front legs, as they enable a rabbit to take off quickly whenever it feels threatened. Interestingly, their back feet have only four toes whereas their front paws have five. The extra toe is called a dewclaw. Rabbits use their dew-claws to help hold on to small items of food.

A rabbit's back paws have four toes, but the front paws have five. Rabbits use the front paws for digging and holding food items.

Where They Live

Rabbits are found in the wild all over the world. More than half of them live in North America—the United States, Canada, and Mexico. There are also species found in parts of South America, Europe, Asia, Africa, and Australia. Rabbits can survive in many different types of **environments**. There are rabbits living on snow-covered plains and rabbits living in

Rabbit species occur all over the world and can thrive in a wide variety of habitats.

wet, swampy areas. They can live in the empty deserts or in busy suburbs where there are scores of people. Most rabbit species, however, are happiest in ordinary woodland settings, such as meadows, forests, and grasslands, particularly where the weather is moderate—not too cold, not too hot—all year long. Rabbits are most commonly found in groups called **warrens**, and they prefer to live in either bowl-shaped nests or in holes in the ground. These holes are called burrows, and the rabbits may dig further tunnels running in several different directions, each leading to a small "room" where they can hide, rest, and care for their young.

Daily Living

Rabbits prefer to carry on their daily business when the sun is either just coming up or just going down. This is the time of day when they feel safest from **predators**, or animals that may attack them. Rabbits are one of the most preyed-upon mammals in the world. They have to always be on the lookout for a huge variety of carnivores (meat-eating animals) including large birds (hawks, eagles, and falcons), wild cats

Rabbits can travel at remarkable speeds. Many other animals hunt them, so they have to be fast!

Rabbits Purr... Kind Of

Rabbits have twenty-eight teeth in total, and those teeth never stop growing. Sometimes they grind their teeth together softly, which produces a sound very similar to a cat's purr. However, a rabbit purring doesn't necessarily mean that it is happy and content. Loud tooth grinding usually means that the rabbit is uncomfortable or in pain.

(lynxes, bobcats, and cougars), wolves and coyotes, and bears. Their long ears are particularly sensitive to threatening noises, such as the sounds of approaching predators, and their large eyes are on constant watch for any signs of danger. When they do sense trouble, they will take off running at incredible speed, often moving in a zigzag pattern to make it harder for a predator to catch them. A frightened rabbit may also use its powerful back legs to pound on the ground as a way of warning other rabbits to flee. When there are no predators around, rabbits will spend most of their time feeding. They are **herbivores**—meaning they eat plants, not other animals—and prefer grasses, weeds, and flowering plants. They are also known to eat a variety of fruits and vegetables, which tends to make farmers think of them as pests.

Lifecycle

Rabbit mothers usually have their babies in the spring, although this can vary depending on what part of the world they're in. A mother will make her nest by digging a hole in the ground—usually in a spot that's well hidden—and cover it with bits of grass, leaves, and sometimes even fur from her own body. The mother can have more than one **litter** of babies during the course of a year. Each litter will have anywhere from four to eight babies, called **kits**, on average. The mother will care for the babies for about one to two months. The kits will then begin to venture out on their own. The average rabbit only lives a few years in the wild, with one to four years being normal.

Trek Talk
A male rabbit is called a buck.
A female is called a doe.

TWO

You Are the Explorer

Rabbits are fairly hardy animals that can live in many different environments. That's good news for you because it means there's a good chance you'll find some close to your home. They are also active all year long (rabbits do not **hibernate**), but your best chance of seeing them is during the warmer months, particularly in the spring. And remember what we learned about their daily **habits**: they usually show themselves when the sun comes up, and again when the sun goes down.

Rabbits do not hibernate in the winter, which means you can find them at any time of the year.

What Do I Wear?

* Old clothes that can get dirty or torn
* Clothes that are also loose-fitting and comfortable
* Shoes or sneakers that won't make too much noise
* A hat
* Sunscreen
* Bug spray

Safari Tip
Don't wear sunglasses on your safari! A rabbit may see a reflection off the lenses and become frightened.

A wild rabbit can be easily identified by its tiny nose, long whiskers, large round eyes, and tall ears.

What Do I Take?

* Binoculars
* Digital camera
* Notebook
* Pen or pencil
* A bag of fresh vegetables
* Snacks
* Drinks

Where Do I Go?

* Along the bottom of fences
* Under hedges and shrubs
* In tall grasses
* At the base of trees
* In and around piles of wood and/or brush
* Near crop rows
* Areas that have become overgrown (such as grass, weeds, or wildflowers)

If you can't find **habitats** such as these on your own property, here are some other safari locations you can try:

* Farms
* Forests
* Meadows
* Hayfields
* Orchards
* Overgrown hillsides

Rabbits are often found in and around farmlands—usually driving farmers crazy by eating their crops!

Safari Tip

It's very important to remember that you should always be with an adult that you trust whenever you go beyond your property. Also, make sure you have permission to continue your safari on someone else's property. You don't want to get into trouble for trespassing!

What Do I Do?

❋ Most importantly, you need to keep quiet and move very slowly. Remember that wild rabbits are very nervous animals and are always on the lookout for any signs of danger. They will become frightened by the sight of a human being and quickly run off. If you are slow with your movements, however, you just might get them to relax and stay where they are.

❋ Have patience. This isn't always easy, because anyone on a rabbit safari wants to see lots of rabbits right away! But the truth is that rabbits spend a lot of their time in hiding, and when they do come out, they don't really want to be seen. It may take some time before you finally see one. In fact, you might even have to go on more than one safari trip before this happens. Also remember that they have very good hearing—so good that they'll hear you long before you see them. You could walk into a field and see nothing where there were five rabbits just a moment earlier!

❋ Stay a safe distance away. When you do see a rabbit or two (or more!), you may have the urge to get as close to it as possible. But if you do this, they won't stick around for long. Once you see one of your furry little friends, you can get a much closer look simply by taking out your **binoculars**. Or, if you prefer, you can use your camera. If the camera has a zoom lens (a

Rabbits are easily frightened, so keep back a safe distance and don't make any sudden, abrupt movements

lens that can help you get a closer look—very much like binoculars do), you can take some great pictures.

❋ If you are lucky enough to find a rabbit hole, but you don't see any rabbits, you can leave a few fresh vegetables just outside the hole or near the nest. Rabbits are particularly fond of carrots, Romaine lettuce, and spinach. Once you've put the vegetables down, you still need to move back a safe distance. If a rabbit smells the vegetables and starts to come forward but then sees you standing there, it will be gone in a flash!

✳ Once you see a rabbit or a group of rabbits, and you feel they are comfortable with you being there, start making some notes in your notebook. Write down anything about the rabbits that seems interesting. What are they doing? Are they eating? If so, what things are they eating? How many rabbits are there? Are

The best results on a rabbit safari come through patience and slow, quiet movements.

Safari Tip

You may have to spread apart some hedge branches, bushes, tall grasses, or weeds in order to find a rabbit hole or nest. If you do, make certain that you don't damage anything. Also, if you need to move something (like a log or a large rock), put it back in the exact spot where it was before you moved it. It might not seem like it matters where things are in the wild, but it does. A natural habitat is a delicately balanced place. If you throw off or disturb one part of it, you can affect all the other parts as well.

there small ones as well as big ones? What colors are they? What time of day is it? What's the weather like? Is it hot? Warm? Cool? Is the ground wet from a recent rainstorm? You might find that all of this information will be very helpful to you on future safaris.

❋ When it's time for you to leave, do so the same way you came: slowly and quietly. And make sure you don't leave anything behind.

✻ When you return home, download any pictures you took and show them to your friends and family. You could also write a more formal journal using both the pictures you took and the notes you made. You could keep an ongoing record of your rabbit safaris from year to year.

Rabbit

Color(s): brown, white, and gray

Location: behind bush

Activity: eating

THREE
A Guide to Rabbits

There are only a few dozen species of rabbits (and their close relatives, hares) in North America, so figuring out which one you've seen on your safari shouldn't be all that difficult. Let's give it a shot.

❋ First, get the notes you scribbled down while you were "in the field" along with those great pictures you took. Next, read through your notes and keep the information floating around in your head. Then, study those pictures very carefully (you only need to focus on one rabbit in particular—whichever one is clearest) and ask the following questions:

Many rabbit species have a whitish tail—this alone may not be enough for you to make a solid identification.

✳ What is the color of the rabbit? How would you describe it?

✳ Does the rabbit have any markings other than its "base" color, such as spots or lines?

✳ How big are the rabbit's hind legs and feet? Rabbits have large back feet, but they're very big on some species.

✳ How long are the ears? Just like the differences in the sizes of the hind feet, some rabbit species have unusually long ears.

Hares are related to rabbits and are characterized by their unusually long ears and slender heads.

✽ How large was the rabbit? If it was very small, it might simply have been young (less than a year old). Then again, a few species in North America never grow very big, even as adults.

✽ Can you see the color of the rabbit's tail? Is it the same color as the rest of the rabbit, or are parts of it vividly white?

Now, go to the next page and see if any of the rabbits in the photos match the **characteristics** that you noted in your answers. Although there are many

When you do see a rabbit, it's a good idea to make notes of what it was doing. This may help you to find more rabbits in the future.

rabbit species in North America, a lot of them look very similar from a distance. This can make them hard to identify. But even if you have trouble, don't get discouraged. Sometimes you can use other information—such as your location (town, state, country) or the exact habitat in which you saw them—to provide the final pieces of your puzzle. Doing a little research on the Internet should also help. Further resources are provided for you in this book's Find Out More section.

Desert Cottontail

Brush Rabbit

Mountain Cottontail

Eastern Cottontail

FOUR

Try This!
Projects You Can Do

Since rabbits live in the wild, you won't be seeing them as often as you would a pet that lives in your house. That doesn't mean you still can't *think* of them as your pets! Once you've gone on enough safari adventures to know where to find the rabbits in your area, you can do all sorts of fun things with them—things that will help them live happier, safer lives. Although you should never get too close to them, try to become familiar with each one that you see. Give them names and make up stories about them in your mind. And remember, throughout all these adventures, always make sure you have an adult with you.

Housecleaning

You probably don't enjoy cleaning up your house, right? But you might enjoy cleaning up the home of your "pet" rabbits in the wild. Rabbits, like any other living thing, need a place to live that presents as few dangers as possible. You can't do anything about wolves, bears, or hawks, but you can do something about trash that's been left behind, either accidentally

Cleaning up a natural environment is a good deed that helps not just rabbits but all wild creatures that live there.

or through carelessness, by other people. If you know of an area near your home where a group of rabbits are living, make a point of going there from time to time and cleaning up any garbage that's lying around. Make sure that you bring a pair of gloves and a bag. You should wear sturdy shoes, too, maybe even a pair of boots. The rabbits might not send you a thank-you note, but they'll appreciate your help all the same.

Pet Rescue

Sometimes rabbits that really are other people's pets get loose and run off into the wild. One easy way to spot such rabbits is by their coloration. Pet rabbits are often pure black, pure white, or some combination of both. Wild rabbits are almost never these colors. If you see a rabbit like this, ask an adult to help you catch it. You can then call the local police department. They should be able to find the rabbit's owners.

Feeding Time

Rabbits eat many different items in the wild, and they are excellent at finding what they need. Still, a little variety never hurts. If you enjoy planting and growing things, then you've got a great little project here. The next time you're at the garden store with your parents, buy a few packets of vegetable seeds (they're very inexpensive). As you learned earlier, rabbits will always be glad to munch on a few carrots, a leaf of Romaine lettuce, or some spinach. Bring the seeds, along with a pair of gloves and a little shovel, to the place where your rabbits live. Loosen some of the dirt, scatter the seeds around, and then cover them up. The vegetables may take some time to grow, but once they do, the rabbits will go crazy over them. If there are any farms nearby, you'll be helping the farmers, too. The rabbits will eat the vegetables you planted instead of the farmers' crops.

Rabbits eat a variety of vegetables, and carrots are among their favorites.

Trek Talk

Rabbits are not only fast runners but also great jumpers. Some can leap as high as 3 feet (1 m)!

Hide Me!

Rabbits are, as you've learned already, very nervous about their safety. They have to be because there are a lot of other animals that hunt them every day. And while they have become very good at finding places to hide, another one or two shelters can't hurt. You could easily make a little shelter out of a cardboard box by cutting a hole in one side for the rabbits to use as a door. But, with the help of an adult (preferably one who is good at building things), you could make an even better one with

27

a little bit of wood and a few nails or screws. Basically, you're looking for a box-shaped shelter with one hole and no floor (remember, rabbits like the dirt). Once your rabbit shelter is done, set it on the ground in the place where your rabbits live. Then make sure you cover it well. Use hay, grass, weeds, branches, or anything that's lying around. Try to cover up everything except the hole so the rabbits can get in and out easily. If you're lucky, they'll find it and start using it.

Since rabbits are preyed upon by so many other animals, they will always appreciate having more places to hide.

Glossary

binoculars	a device that helps you to see things that are very far away
burrow	a hole in the ground where wild rabbits live, often with more than one tunnel and several "rooms"
carnivore	an animal that eats the meat and flesh of other animals
characteristic	a specific trait or quality that an animal has, such as tan fur or brown eyes
environment	the general type of place where an animal lives, such as a forest, swamp, or desert
habit	the normal activities of an animal
habitat	the exact type of place in which an animal lives, such as a burrow, cave, or shoreline
hibernate	a period of rest during cold months
herbivore	an animal that only eats plants
kit	a baby rabbit
litter	a group of young animals born at one time
predator	an animal that will attack and eat another one
shelter	a place where an animal can go inside
species	one particular type of animal
warren	a community of rabbits

Find Out More

Books

Macken, JoAnn Early. *Jackrabbits.* New York: Weekly Reader, 2009.

Marsico, Katie. *Rabbits: How Do We Live Together?* North Mankato, MN: Cherry Lake Publishing, 2010.

Robbins, Lynette. *Rabbits and Hares.* New York: PowerKids Press, 2011.

Websites

National Geographic's Cottontail Rabbit Page

animals.nationalgeographic.com/animals/mammals/cottontail-rabbit/

Basic information on one of the most common rabbits in the world, along with photos, fast facts, and a map.

Wild Rabbit Facts

rabbitempire.org/wild-rabbit-facts

A long list of interesting factoids about wild rabbits from the Rabbit Empire website—including a few photos.

Rabbit Facts—What to Do

pleasebekind.com/rabbit.html

The Please Be Kind website has a great amount of helpful information for anyone who discovers rabbits that they feel are in any kind of danger or trouble. Many practical suggestions, lots of rabbit facts, contact information (which should not be used without an adult's permission), and links to other pages can be found on this website.

Index

Page numbers in **boldface** are illustrations.

About the Author

WIL MARA is an award-winning author of more than 140 books. He began his writing career with several titles about herpetology, the study of reptiles and amphibians. He has since branched out into other subject areas and continues to write educational books for children. To find out more about Mara and his work, you can visit his website at www.wilmara.com.